SIDEBROW BOOKS

The Courier's Archive & Hymnal

Published by Sidebrow Books
P.O. Box 86921
Portland, OR 97286
sidebrow@sidebrow.net
www.sidebrow.net

Cover art by Ryan McLennan ("Fit for the Table")
Cover & book design by Jason Snyder

-     ISBN: 0-9814975-9-4
ISBN-13: 978-0-9814975-9-4

FIRST EDITION | FIRST PRINTING
9 8 7 6 5 4 3 2 1
SIDEBROW BOOKS 010
PRINTED IN THE UNITED STATES

Sidebrow Books titles are distributed by
Small Press Distribution

Titles are available directly from Sidebrow at
www.sidebrow.net/books

A Member of
Inter
section
incubator
Services for Artists
www.theintersection.org

Sidebrow is a member of the Intersection Incubator, a program of
Intersection for the Arts (www.theintersection.org) providing fiscal
sponsorship, incubation, and consulting for artists. Contributions
to Sidebrow are tax-deductible to the extent allowed by law.

Chicago IL
July 19, 2014

The Courier's Archive & Hymnal

JOSHUA MARIE WILKINSON

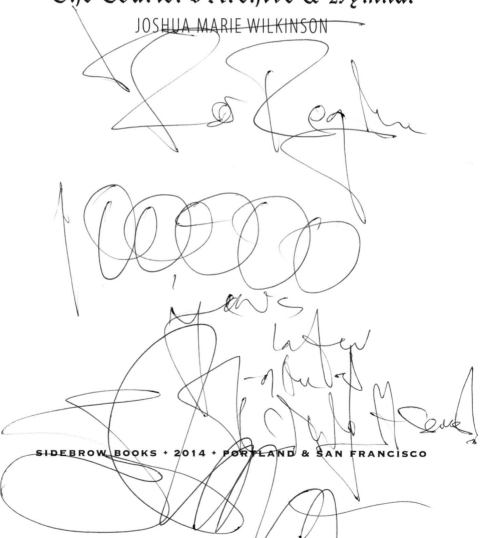

For Regan

10000 years later

SIDEBROW BOOKS • 2014 • PORTLAND & SAN FRANCISCO

Acknowledgments

I thank the editors of the journals in which excerpts of this work first appeared, in different forms: *American Letters & Commentary*; *Eleven Eleven*; *Lana Turner: A Journal of Poetry and Opinion*; *Mid-American Review*; *New Delta Review*; *Poor Claudia*; and *Verse*.

An excerpt of "The Dogs" was published as part of the Poem-A-Day series by the Academy of American Poets, and the first paragraph of "Day for Night for Night" was printed as a broadside for the So-and-So Reading Series in Raleigh, North Carolina.

"In the Trade of Alive Letters Mis-sent" was published as a chapbook by Brave Men Press (Northampton, 2011), an excerpt of which was also printed as a broadside by New Michigan Press to commemorate a reading at the Poetry Center in Tucson, Arizona.

A warm thank you to all the editors and printers, especially Shane Smith, Ander Monson, E.B. Goodale, & Brian Foley. And to my friends & family: Solan Jensen, David Rubin, Aurelie Sheehan, Jane Miller, Alison Hawthorne Deming, NEG, Smithy, Brandon Shimoda, Dot Devota, ZBS, Baby Snakes, Peter Streckfus, Kate & Brent, FS&G, & Chris Cokinos. Jason, John, Kris, and Zuzu: thank you, Sidebrow.

Italicized lines on pages 5 & 7 are from Bashō's *The Narrow Road to the Deep North and Other Travel Sketches* (tr. Nobuyuki Yuasa), on which this book is based. The italicized sentence on page 27 is from Samuel Beckett's *Molloy*.

The Courier's Archive & Hymnal is Book 3 of the *No Volta* pentalogy.

For the Pond

They were offered the choice between becoming kings or the couriers of kings. The way children would, they all wanted to be couriers.

—Franz Kafka (tr. Clement Greenberg)

Day for Night for Night

Dragging a long hull—& following the debased coinage of ancients—I blocked through the consumptive river, looking into a wood grown huge without kings or their servants, cutting doors from oaks.

Night stalled wet with gulls against mission islands. A corduroy song I could holler into the ghost maze. Commands of a body to falter.

A long, weird sleep under dripping boughs, my breath a gold cloud puffed into rabbits. & from my dream, the token used for a bathtub stopper.

Fog lolling at a bend where the ravine shunts to weed. River's edge a brain of mica, claimed for ice melt.

It sucked off my boot, & I tossed the other into a hollow.

Bird-raked wind, laudanum in my tea, & my mouth cut by a scrappy branch.

Loops of rain trafficking in the sooty tent of deciduous half-ceiling. A seeming doorway through ivy hung like netting & nests. I follow your dents out of here.

With a polaroid of Matta-Clark's hand-drawn labyrinth taped to my satchel.

How did the song stake out a clearing? What icy star kept you to yourself? The rider phantom's beside me now, listening with an accordion's wheeze for breath.

Night carpets over.

A scene before my eyes: lake mist over three girls triangulating a tarp to wrap their mother, dead.

Steel trap of the lake topped with snow & waves wound to hooks by stagnated wind. A blast furnace gathers wraiths to statue up.

False horizon of bony light where the moon stutters a beam onto our bridge. Fields rippled with lime, a crow drops onto a tractor seat for seed. Four thousand entries toward heaven papered over the clapboard walls of the diarist's pond shed.

& a stalkerish moon into a clearing spelled which travelers' shadows were still here.

I met Samuel Beckett & held a cap he'd taken
from the head of one of his actors to shoo mice
into the theater alley while he tied his sneaker &
repeated my full name finding a sort of song in
it. I put this into my voice recorder. Minus is the
one I gave it to. You may find him in a studio
apartment in one of the western cities.

Doing certain tasks with voices, he threads
American grids with their muttering in his
skeleton.

Dark archive, what is your name for no becoming,
stammering through wind?

(Clean your arms up with a rag & slow the way
down to flies.)

Your man gets his dogs together on the nettlepath,
where each stranger shows his face in bordering
light.

Tonight just opened its door. Your stranger steps in with a head of worries: saying, I have no feeling in my hands, my face. *The last brother, the moon's ditch.* We sketched the map out together with red tea. I held my hand open for him to practice the lines on.

Sorry I know you less than the ice does.

Mr. Matta-Clark, dawn sniffs through an oval, mooring the joists. Which are the tools for chronicling what you sawed through? Drywall in an elbow crease, scraped free with sink water.

A hole smeared into the boathouse floor. I startle the gull-laden ocean into beams.

Your brother stood into the window, river below like animals waiting. Bored gleaming spits through a net you turned the boathouse into. A short grin in your work saw awake.

Toting your cameras down to the work of dust underground.

The train conductor stutters at a silvery flask, & night unloads its poisonous spores. I touched the door's window with my glove off. Pigeons in the spikes anyhow. A woman reading "Passers-by" with an eye shut, her wrist marked blue. Snow comes early for the city streets, & the trees yield to what signals?

Incorporation is no enemy we fold our hands around as though it were a cat's head. A bog's our northerly quorum.

Fire sleeves, summer graves, & the dead woman points the way. Then roof hens flap under a half-moon. Golden deerhounds stand sentry. Cobble rows, skeletal slavering. Trappers mend the damaged traps.

Ink about the throat of the sleepwalker lured to hovering lamp moths.

Your fox asked again for the road-weary ones to collect in the sewergrate shadows at a bit of lightning. To strike set in a cache of stage directions penciled onto the curtain tags.

A bit of stubble's on the paw where fur was caught, but your bones are alright, fox.

Slowly under music: a feint, a sleight of hand, a story of snow insulating the bivouac melting over a campfire's low flickering. Scenes where moving pictures had stilled.

We could photograph the shadows & cordon them into a book with our miniature camera. We could turn the pages with our healed hands.

Stars tipped to their levers & rats along the twine built a periphery.

Milking the handle of an axe, corpsethieves steady each other into a corridor.

The sleepwalkers molt in the clearing. Their steam rises, cottony. Covered in fallen coin, they fled to the held-open paths.

Eyes gritted with wind, what are you looking to have found?

Whose hand are you holding out & for what?

The summer graves alive with lavender at the sea edge. A hollow choir careening over a pedal steel until a treadle gets the white outside to nudge open a door.

Pier hounds working the eels here.

Fat oars offset sea foam jagging the pillowy
shore. I hold the ceiling up with the meat of my
underhand. Lighthouse misting a searcher for
stars. Airy breakers yanked by tempest masters.

At this window, I track the tide's retreat one
buoy per crash. To drag thunder toward my vat
of white beer. A stripling on the marsh crag,
listening in his rubber boots.

Where'd you learn your stony knock?

Your hithering gets the blood to cadence. A nurse
at the net mender's ear with invisible talk.

Clouds above uncoiling rope to the world's black
socket. My fingers ground to a cartoon glow, as
the ocean roils yellow & gauges dock the moon.

Cold satellite, who will loll you down to a sandy
beach?

No charms left to shake off this arrhythmia, as if
a love would return from without. How weather
knows the bent earth.

Doddering beyond sleep, the messenger girl now
casts pocket stones from the man's tweed jacket
at trains passing.

Viaducts grew from noise settling a leveled city
block. The child unclenched her fingers from the
man's as if from a doorknob.

Spidery calls ash around us. A memory splits
open its shine.

Great street holes had buckled the tenement's ground floor till the city listed & gave off an armory of scents contagious. I waited for things to unlatch & ease themselves apart.

Drawn to stories of escape, the question now was not even *toward what*, but instead *which path out?*

My phone's gleam throws a little bastard net around the keyhole.

I want one thing handed over to me. An injured gull placed in newspaper on the tabletop.

What were the good myths about? Not merely desire. & not just forbidden desire either, exactly: but some slant choice recasting the future freshly black.

The moon spots us with its lacquer. I dream out huge staircases, wooden & mossy. A phone booth's ringing glass clamps us to it.

Nightfall motion detecting lights pop on. Winter grooms its stagehands.

Rats do their work. Work avails its rats. Ivy residue hoarders line up against the trellis.

We rig into the loam with our spades, simple picks.
My father called the land out of our names. Offal
& its attendants. Another us to batter about.

Echoes learn the gridwork & send out their
pings.

I go alone with a dead farthing: not my only friend,
but my enemy's lone enemy yet to debase.

Sleet brightening the garden's own fogs.

You hold the words against your mouth. The
sounds come out each in a little squeak.

Mice clamber onto the shoulders of the messenger girl—*shush* of her slippers—sleepwalking up the cellar steps.

They skitter like little door knockers. Her eyes are fishy with ice, as a puddle from the dripping faucet draws her into the kitchen where your stranger waits at the table, watching the kettle work to a boil.

Moonlight's bundled in cords of wet wood out there.

In the Trade of Alive Letters Mis-sent

History is a series of apologies, unmet by the eyes of the forced-down—a cold donor of blood in search of a talker to listen with.

Skunks in the yard teemed to shrubs as snowy slop fell against the sky's foundry. I hold the lantern. You hold my hand not holding the lantern. The moon flinches, flickers. We right ourselves versus the hedge of glowworms, & loosen stalks from the thresher. To shuffle over the roseate passenger bridgeworks with a flashlight for dome light.

A crease in the field where foxes slow to gauze. White fetid wind over the other carriers of lanterns & manured soil. I start the story like the roof of a pilled house.

Candle to mouse eye to a watery match flame transcribed into red radar blips learning our whereabouts from beyond.

The eye into scope, with a gift we fold: halving at a distance, under the downed jet's wing wobble. A fog dense as cheese, yet we took ourselves into it. Dealing in the trade of alive letters mis-sent, a burlap bag in the basket of the courier's bicycle.

The house number revealed to its marrow. Out along our river. Yellow crops cotton the eye. A sort of station or congress in the woods, concealing a hole in the rent fence.

Tracks thread the coastline with trains. Hymns for the couriers' bridge & the couriers. We sang to the city under a swatch of chimney flue ash.

Badly limned houses stack the boulevard. Canopy of smog trussing the unanointed. Draughts of soiled flyleaf light. You go here. I go too, until tonight. Then the strategy racks its herd. I say, let's slow to creek speed. Awe is a lesson for getting pond-still in the brain. Standing water drains us through to a chamber & so our little poems draw open what follows:

Shadows find a herdpath to the overlook.

Poems composed in the battle night: island isthmus photographed as an uncoiled jetty.

I ask the dogs for a name against motel coolant dripping onto the carpets. Where what's hidden in the courier's satchel visits you at your mirror.

Sapling, could you follow me with your switch if the story gets too—?

Poems levered out in a field below four stars & the limpsey moon: a wad of lavender in my jaw.

The girls drop a compass into their kettle against bears. Carriers of lanterns holding the planets off like mosquitoes.

Shutters, what do you have against light?

The Dogs

I must have fallen asleep, for all of a sudden there was the moon, a huge moon framed in the window. This is how the roomers let grief in, as through a timed sieve. It goes both ways between window glass. Chords of bickering light. Chokehold of a brother on a brother. Each animal sigh into the basin of dusk.

I hold the dream back with a smoke wall. Staple the city up one delivery at a time. Sirens last in the brain, trickling through the movie's thrash. A woman pulling her stockings off in the entry when her mother comes down the stairs to unlock the door & let me in.

What I am trying to photograph stalls out, pastes itself to the sun-bleached poster of the shop.

Dusting what phantoms scour furniture for. Little death for a sailor wishing the sea from his chest.

I go holding the rain up with a black umbrella
in the rubbled season here, among kings known
never to touch a door.

Will you open the iron gate to the small quarry
become garden? Catullus to Quintilian, stabbed
on a train by daylight through faulty curtains.
Debauched land from our lord in its rightful
quadrant & decade.

Feeling through the darker paths with my bird
set, I let the dogs flow loose into the rivery sedge.
You may have my word to use against yours.

Hold still for mice to take hold.

Battery of cliff swallows parting above an ataxic leaving the bridge shelter's cardboard residence.

Cement boathouse through which gulls got scent of carp drying on the quays.

I, too, have been erased by the traveler's moon.

Stood as though listening to a starling in the ceiling, a thief gets to the wall or becomes it. A net big enough to catch a child, but not strong enough to carry one, waits on the bed of the truancy officer's truck.

The removed are now simply housed under a spate of viaducts.

Stood in the muddy shoals for hours where they culled for what the anchor had been attached to.

The little ghost of your poem stands up as a faked emblem, marking a placeholder in the lot.

The motel's second sign was lit, sending us back to the highway's roadblock crew. Plastic handles of suitcases cold, snow onto the windshield hot. Hand-drawn hands on the flooring under the mats, a crossbones skeleton makes its business known. A man's shorn whiskers in the sink of the lobby washroom, otherwise spotless. Save who comes to the door with a question.

So I stand, a muskmelon awaiting your machete.

Will what lingers follow you through the carpet?

I failed to see the cut as an entry, the joke too as
an apology.

I turned to head back. A droplight hung from the
eaves, spun a shadow down in the form of mine
& I watched there a moment for the courier's
trail.

What's not me falters or, like grass, bends back up
to shake in the airs.

Discovery's truncheoned themes & phone cable
skeining the so-called horizon: what is there left
to find out that has not been laid into a plot &
mixed over?

What of the cold did you bring inside here.

What of the land could you carry off in your eye?

Haggard saint considers the doorbell, & this is where I hold the phone to my chest.

Steady comes the messenger plunking her slate rocks to cross.

You're not you here?

Your blithe skeleton shadows inside you.

I follow the whistle of the lantern carrier's bridegroom out. A droplight, an orange cord I took for a snake was the line to the pond shed.

What force to pulley on the moon.

This is the story of children using an old door for
a plank to the house across their alleyway.

Snow off the branches pulled to cyclones.

Blindness of being partway down the stairs.

The truancy officer locks the door of his pickup.
The messenger girl begins to copy her translation
by hand. Birds explode by. He says, Stand down,
little courier. First, show me what's in your hand,
she says. & so a trade begins.

Seasons dissolve, divulge water, clock us, & spin
out.

I carry their song in the wax of an apple.

Your whereabouts remain with you.

What satellite did you mistake for being heard?

Into which era did you think you'd reappear?

(Your city stuffed into a breadbox.)

Two kinds of animals fix us to the earth: the indefatigable & the snared off.

She spit into an unslashed meadow for luck.

The shower drain is a passage for rats, but I work to forget this with my hair shampooed into a sailboat.

We smoked cloves behind the 7-11.

Right there, where they'd winched the stenographer's car from the cape reeds. They shot it day for night for night.

Dug the vein out finally on the fourth attempt.

Awake enough to draw myself through the emergency doors.

A new hole in my face in the dream. Nettle tea, numbed to the enamel.

Aphids at the tomato vines betwixt the firing squad having coffee.

Alms of: here's a little dead bird I stored in a cabinet for you.

Dogyard bristling. Something on its hind legs at the mail slot.

Steady comes the messenger:

Curls loosen about her forehead as the sweat breaks. A sprig of lilac you held for how long.

Sky polishes the cars. The plastic owl returns under the arm of our hero's dead twin.

She repeats *egress* & *ingress* over the lobby scuffle.

The bellhop's wrist was bandaged with napkins.

The elevator goes up for a long time before returning with nobody.

A ridge of pollen drawn clean into the vent. Trail of gumdrops shows our courier where went a friend.

The bats follow you to the tavern & wait outside on your bicycle until the tenth inning.

Rain rocks the dead.

Curtain, I say: please come down now.

The ocean bedspreads back to reveal our logged trash. Chronicle of falling & rising with condensation.

The delivery's insignia vouchsafed to the underboot of the courier.

A drawknife holds its lovely shape when pulled.

So you followed a sparrow into an empty shop.

The dead child uprights herself & smoothes her dress in weird smears. A candle winnows the room down to a mouth. I study the window, the way it follows those who exit into the weather. My eye breathes in the horizon, dreaming wallpaper into rain's spitty patterns.

A carrier of lice to rid the king of his washers.

The sky's winding sheet. A lukewarm pill.

Our publican smokes at the entry, standing with a fieldmouse. His song somehow rhyming lead, shortening, lard, & peony.

The ocean floor is slower than it looks.

Stood under the gutter spouts to better know the monsoon.

Is it improved out in the clouds auditioning you for trees?

A callous, my pact, so I'm holding it out.

How the day lengthens its coat for those you forgot: stenciled arrows on the alley wall, dropped my shirt in a wadded ball down a well & came home from without.

But the moths find you, phantom. & they flit up at the crackle of the javelinas in the wash.

So, you know the ground here? Where else is new or to you called unknown? Gumtree tipping onto the marsh meadow's shoreline.

What armors the birds?

The apology wends off as smoke ground to gravel. So you were here alright, coughing on the live tape.

What snare won't bring you back a friend?

A cat pretending to not follow you into the arrowed alley—your future death's become a pathway:

Bridge witness captioned in the newsbox for three quarters. Shrikes now follow the moon off.

Black ants, you're alright crating your sugar & shit into the night's stone vacuum. Is that all you can carry? Is what you're part of knowable up here?

Who's on my kitchen floor asleep tonight? That would be snakes.

All this bad falling light is a trope for what, staying put? Getting the dead out of the dust? Stagnant pools of offal, alright.

Isn't that what we've come to close our eyes around? The bridge is a means for crossing.

Then why are you stopping, little sentry?

They dropped children down sewer holes in the street as the bombs lit off.

What else, rain?

Yes, rain.

What else, more rain?

Yes & more.

Each of the staples pulled from the din by the remover of staples.

To each saint his own rabbit, shade, acolyte, & contract.

Ascending planes lured coyote across the gravel.

We swam up under the tipped-over boat for a pocket of air to find one another.

The truancy officer begins by checking the tavern's fridges. He stubs his cigarette out on the banister & turns a dime on his thumb. The hollow trees house various things in the fable: homemade weapons from foliage, the bank clerk's pen on a chain crinkling in your shirt pocket.

Tied to your belt loop, was it?

A bit of thieving to remind your blood what it tracks like. Leapt off of Phantoms Cave, as from the paperback's cover. They'd climbed the gully line to a break of scotch broom.

Your man smears his apron with friendly ease.

What the flue catches, you know, gets a little path into your home.

See, souls coalesce, just don't say it aloud or loudly in your breath. Children draw their foals into a cabbagey row. I sound out among the other moths.

Hold down the fortress for a minute. I have to pick up my little brother. & your little brother. & your little brother & yours & yours & the dogs.

Fortnight's Insignia

to endorse the dust
shall not add to your bounty

—Samuel Beckett

Go soundly, soft harmonium drag. The temper
is a stockade. The vestibule is a spot to get us off
if you've been clamped down. Have you now?
Come inside to hear of it, but speak clear & slow
for the tape to coil you in—I'll need this later for
a transcription.

Now to the hinge of memory, the dropper of
orange cough syrup, & a flat file for the wall safe.
What are your tools & how do you secure them
to your person? Clicking one lamp off fastens
shadows to each other, but that's the trick you
taught me. Lepers Boat Creek, they call it—its
apostrophe also wiped free.

So, the little courier grows dud wings & can't lift
off. Isn't that how you want it to end? Devoured
by a wolf pack after they looked so docile at the
river?

The lobby's lone attendant twins to Warhol's Elvis
cowboys in the hall's double mirror. Sounds of
fucking in room 304 & we're in room 305. So it's
gonna be that kind of century. The ducts blasting.
The window onto a window onto a supper fight.
Snow twisting traffic into a V.

The ocean chopper's hunting for ice on which
to land. Now pull the dead pilot's gear off his
head. Do we take his wallet, too? What do we
hide in plain sight? The worst of it won't sow into
broadcasts.

Fledgling pilot, your days are soon to end. The
storm's indifference is a vehicle. That funnel is
only its shape from a satellite learning your face.

What you see will peel the paint from the dead
detective's glass door:

Fortnight's insignia & Twombly's cape shadows
dragged across the plain. Birds lift from the
cataract, a pool of stars.

A winter month's short door through which to
crawl.

Underground now with a heaven of storm water
called runoff by the above.

I hold the map up & speak into the forming ice
for an echo to crunch back.

Joshua Marie Wilkinson lives in Tucson, Arizona.

SIDEBROW BOOKS | www.sidebrow.net

SIDEBROW 01 ANTHOLOGY
*A multi-threaded, collaborative
narrative featuring work by 65 writers*
SB001 | ISBN: 0-9814975-0-0

WHITE HORSE
*A collaborative narrative featuring
poetry and prose by 25 writers*
SB006 | ISBN: 0-9814975-5-1

ON WONDERLAND
& WASTE
Sandy Florian
Collages by Alexis Anne Mackenzie
SB002 | ISBN: 0-9814975-1-9

LETTERS TO
KELLY CLARKSON
Julia Bloch
SB007 | ISBN: 0-9814975-6-X

SELENOGRAPHY
Joshua Marie Wilkinson
Polaroids by Tim Rutili
SB003 | ISBN: 0-9814975-2-7

SPED
Teresa K. Miller
SB008 | ISBN: 0-9814975-7-8

CITY
Featuring work from The City Project
SB004 | ISBN: 0-9814975-3-5

BEYOND THIS POINT
ARE MONSTERS
Roxanne Carter
SB009 | ISBN: 0-9814975-8-6

NONE OF THIS IS REAL
Miranda Mellis
SB005 | ISBN: 0-9814975-4-3

FOR ANOTHER
WRITING BACK
Elaine Bleakney
SB011 | ISBN: 1-940090-00-8

To order, and to view information on new and forthcoming titles,
visit www.sidebrow.net/books.